HOW DOES
IT GROW?

OAK TREE

Jinny Johnson

Illustrations by Graham Rosewarne

FRANKLIN WATTS
LONDON•SYDNEY

An Appleseed Editions book

First published in 2009 by Franklin Watts
338 Euston Road, London NW1 3BH

Franklin Watts Australia
Hachette Children's Books
Level 17/207 Kent St, Sydney, NSW 2000

© 2009 Appleseed Editions

Created by Appleseed Editions Ltd,
Well House, Friars Hill, Guestling,
East Sussex TN35 4ET

Designed by Helen James
Edited by Mary-Jane Wilkins
Picture research by Su Alexander

ISBN 978 0 7496 8789 2

Dewey Classification: 582.16

A CIP catalogue for this book is available from the British Library.

Photograph acknowledgements
Page 9 George Holland/Photolibrary Group; 19 Richard Packwood/
Photolibrary Group; 25 SGM SGM/Photolibrary Group;
29 Dennis Flaherty/Photolibrary Group
Front cover Dennis Flaherty/Photolibrary Group

Printed in China

Franklin Watts is a division of Hachette Children's Books,
an Hachette Livre UK company.
www.hachettelivre.co.uk

Contents

A small start   4

Beginning to grow   6

What the oak needs   8

Growing bigger   10

The tree trunk   12

Home in a tree   14

Autumn   16

Winter   18

Spring   20

Oak flowers   22

Summer   24

Starting again   26

More about oak trees   28

Words to remember   30

Index   32

A small start

Trees are the **biggest** of all **living things**. But they start small. A tall **oak tree** grows from a **nut** called an **acorn**.

The acorn holds the oak tree's seed. It has **a tough shell** and it sits in a **neat cup**. The cup is attached to the oak branch by a stalk.

Acorns **ripen in late summer** and fall from the tree. Inside each acorn is enough **food** for a **tiny tree** to start growing.

SOME BIRDS LIKE TO EAT ACORNS.

How does the acorn start to grow?

Beginning to grow

The **hard shell** of the acorn splits
open and a **tiny root** appears.
The root grows **down into the
earth** to hold the plant upright.

Next, a stem called a **shoot**
grows up from the acorn
and the **first leaves** appear.

The leaves of the oak are large
and have **toothed edges**.

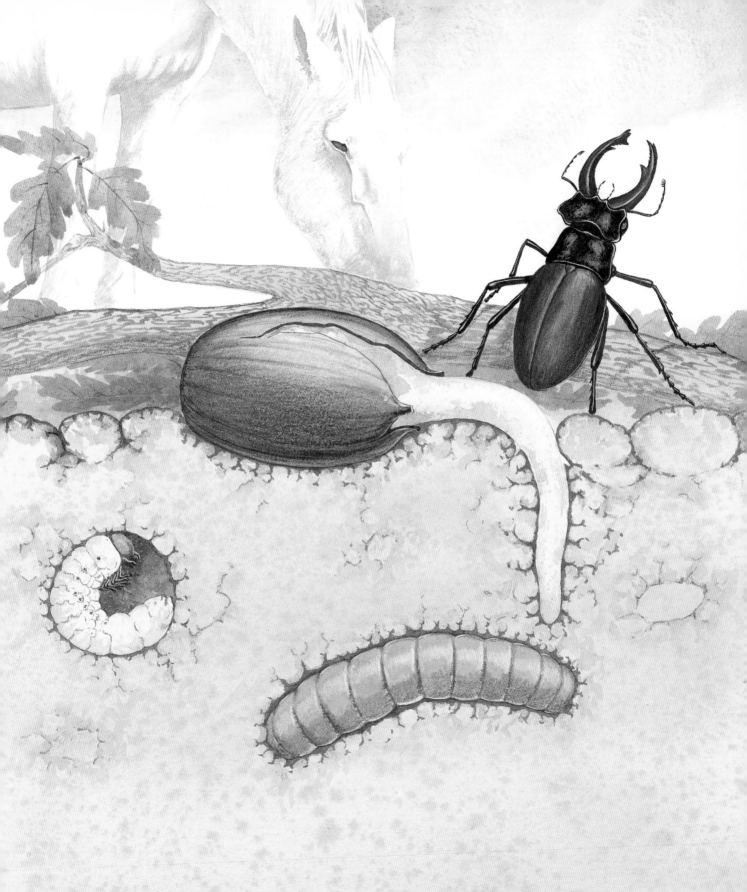

What does the plant need to help it grow?

What the oak needs

Like all **plants**, an oak tree
needs **water** and **sunlight**
to help it grow.

Plants make their own food.
The **green leaves** use water,
sunlight and a gas called
carbon dioxide in the air
to **make their food**.

The food helps plants **grow**
more **leaves** on their branches
and more **roots** underground.

THE FIRST LITTLE
LEAVES OF AN
OAK TREE.

How long does it take for an oak tree to grow?

Growing bigger

During its **first year** the oak plant grows **taller** and taller. Many more leaves appear. Its **stem** is still thin and **spindly**.

During the **second year** the stem starts to grow into a woody **trunk**. It takes about **20 years** for an oak to grow from an **acorn** into a **tree**.

The tree gets **bigger** and grows new **branches** for many more years. Oak trees can live for **hundreds of years**.

What is the tree trunk like?

The tree trunk

The **tree trunk** has to be very **strong** to support all the branches and leaves. As the tree **grows**, the trunk becomes **fatter** and fatter.

The tree **trunk** has a rough covering called **bark**. The bark is like the tree trunk's skin and **protects** the inside from the weather and damage.

Lots of **insects live** on the tree trunk. Some are almost the **same colour** so they are very **hard to see**.

CAN YOU SPOT THE MOTH HIDING ON THIS OAK TREE TRUNK?

Which animals live in oak trees?

Home in a tree

An oak tree is home to lots of creatures. **Birds** make **nests** in the branches. **Squirrels** live in **holes** in the trunk.

Insects such as **butterflies** perch on the leaves and **beetles** scurry around on the **bark**.

Bigger creatures such as **foxes, skunks** and **badgers** dig dens under the roots of a large tree.

LOOK AT ALL THE CREATURES LIVING IN THIS TREE.

What happens to the oak tree in autumn?

Autumn

In autumn the **days** grow **shorter** and the weather becomes **colder**. There is **less sunlight** to help the tree make food. The leaves **change colour**.

They turn **brown** or **red** and begin to **fall** to the **ground**. Slowly they **rot** into the earth.

Oak trees **lose** their **leaves** so they are protected from the **cold**. If the leaves stayed on the trees they could **freeze** and harm the tree.

What happens in the winter?

Winter

In winter the oak tree's **branches** are **bare**. After the leaves fall from the tree in the autumn the tree **rests**.

Most of the **birds** have left the tree, but there may be squirrels **sheltering** in **holes** in the trunk.

Look carefully and you will see **tiny buds** on the **twigs**. They are growing bigger, ready to open into new **leaves** in **spring**.

AN OAK TREE
IN THE MIDDLE
OF WINTER.

When does the tree wake up again?

Spring

The tree **wakes** from its winter rest in spring. The **buds** on the oak tree start to open into fresh **green leaves**.

The **days** are **longer** now and there is **more sunlight**. The leaves can start to make **food** again.

Birds come back to the tree and start to make **nests** among the **leafy branches**.

When do the flowers grow?

Oak flowers

Soon the oak tree's **flowers** appear. There are both **male** and **female** flowers.

The male flowers are **long** and **straggly** and are called **catkins**. They are covered in **yellow dust** called **pollen**. The pollen is light and **blows away** in the wind.

When pollen reaches the **female flowers** they can make seeds. The female flowers grow at the **tips** of the **twigs** and are smaller than the catkins.

When does the tree grow acorns?

Summer

In summer the female **flowers** start to **grow** into **acorns**. One part becomes the **nut** and another part is the acorn **cup**.

An **oak** tree doesn't make acorns until it is about **50 years old**. Some years an oak might have **50,000** acorns. Other years it has far **fewer**.

Even when there are thousands of acorns, only **a few** will grow into oak **trees**.

What happens to all the acorns?

Starting again

Birds such as **crows** and **pigeons** pick acorns from the branches. **Mice, pigs** and **deer** gobble them up under the tree. **Squirrels** pick up acorns and **hide them** away to eat later.

Most acorns are eaten and many young plants are **trampled** on or **eaten** while they are still small.

Next **spring** one or two **acorns** will start to grow into big beautiful **oak trees**, like their parent tree. Eventually they too will grow acorns to make more trees.

More about oak trees

Where do oak trees grow?

There are many different kinds of oak tree. They grow in Europe, Asia and in both North and South America. Most oaks are deciduous, which means they lose their leaves in autumn and grow new ones that open the following spring. Some oaks are evergreen. Most have leaves with toothed edges.

Spreading seeds

Oaks are wind pollinated. The male flowers, called catkins, produce lots of tiny pollen grains. These are blown by the wind to fertilize the female flowers which grow on the same tree. The female flowers then produce nuts called acorns, which contain seeds.

Many animals eat acorns, so the nuts may be carried some distance away from the parent tree. Here there may be more sunlight and space, to help the young saplings grow into mature trees.

A MATURE OAK TREE
IN MIDSUMMER.

Words to remember

acorn

A nut that grows on an oak tree. It contains the tree's seeds.

bark

The outer covering of a tree's trunk and branches.

bud

The part of a plant that grows into a leaf or flower.

carbon dioxide

A gas in the air that plants use to make food.

catkin

A type of flower that grows on oak trees and some other kinds of tree.

pollen

Tiny powdery grains made by flowers.

shoot

New growth on a plant.

trunk

The woody main stem of a tree.

twig

A small branch that may carry leaves, buds and flowers.

Websites

Wild Film History
http://www.wildfilmhistory.org/film/305/clip/459/
Life+and+death+of+an+oak+tree.html

BBC
http://www.bbc.co.uk/gardening/gardening_with_children/
homegrownprojects_tree.shtml

Woodland Trust
http://www.naturedetectives.org.uk/

Index

acorns 4, 5, 6, 7, 10, 24, 25,
    26, 27, 28, 30
animals 7, 11, 13, 14, 15, 18,
    26, 27, 28

bark 12, 13, 14, 15, 30
birds 4, 5, 14, 15, 20, 21,
    23, 26
branches 4, 5, 10, 12, 13,
    18, 19, 20, 21, 26
buds 18, 20, 30

catkins 22, 23, 28, 30

flowers 21, 22, 23, 24, 28

insects 7, 12, 13, 14, 15, 23

leaves 6, 7, 8, 9, 10, 11, 12, 13,
    14, 15, 16, 18, 20, 21, 28, 29

pollen 22, 28, 30

roots 6, 7, 8, 14

shoots 6, 31
stem 10, 11, 31
sunlight 8, 16, 20, 28

trunk 11, 12, 13, 14, 15,
    18, 31
twigs 18, 22, 23, 31